JOURNAL

JOURNAL

John DesCamp

Wind Mountain Press

Portland, Oregon

ISBN: 979-8-218-16742-4

Wind Mountain Press
P.O. Box 4448
Portland, OR 97208

www.johndescamp.com

Printed in the United States of America.

Contents

Journey's End / 105

Epilogue / 121

Colophon / 123

Acknowledgements

Once again (he says it will be the last time) my editor and good friend Dennis Stovall has not only provided the photos on the front and back of the book, but has given me his constructive advice and patient wisdom in helping me shape the poems in this book and in shaping the book itself. This book has been a partnership between the two of us and wouldn't have come together without him.

Jim Halliday's photography makes visible the feelings that underly the writing. Ten years ago, at the insistence of a mutual friend, I called and introduced myself to Jim. My friend promised me that Jim was an extraordinary person who would enrich my life. He was right. And for the last 10 years I have had the great pleasure to be one of Jim's friends and to be able to include his photographs in my books.

Not long after we met, Jim contracted a difficult form of cancer. His response was to double down on the joyful life he was living—his love of his wife Karen and his family, his music, his small but exquisite vineyard and wines, photography, gardening, good food, acting, community service and, every day, passing along his joy and wisdom to everyone he met.

Jim left us last year, and the world seems a lesser place without him. But he will always live in the hearts of his friends.

This book is dedicated to Dennis and Jim: for me, and for this book, *conditii sine qua non*.

In My Beginning Is My End

January Sunday Walk

Gray ridged clouds above the river—
the ribs of a skinny greyhound.

Ducks and geese pairing—
feathered side-long glances.

Ceanothus, catkins,
the willow bark an angry red

Like a child holding its breath
waiting for Spring.

New Year's Haiku

Chrysanthemum moon
white contrail in blue black sky
melancholy joy.

Pinto

Pinto puppy
languid sausage friend
play, lick, eat, sleep
life is what it is
then black mist falls.

Winter Solstice

Dad was a hundred and eight today. His ashes
reside at Mt. Calvary;
his spirit elsewhere—
sometimes in our hearts
when we have room for something there
besides ourselves

Through the cemetery gate
we arrive with the unrisen sun
black green shadowed grass
under a fine film of frost
speechless patient headstones
march raggedly uphill while
we crunch along beside them

Each year it's the same comfortable ritual
we clean his headstone, then
anoint it with whisky
ourselves as well
and talk with him for a while
he's an active part of the conversation
nothing's ever resolved, of course
but it's necessary to cover
the familiar ground again
just to be sure
nothing has been forgotten

The sun erupts behind
the black trees at the top of the hill
as if to say
new light will, truly,
follow this darkness

Equinox

Dry boards breathe new rain;
sharp smell of dust. Summer dies
giving birth to autumn.

Ouroboros

Down an ancient stone stairway
in the basement of the universe
He sits, bathed in the eternal light
and everlasting darkness of creation.

From His yellow cushion
He sees them all: the never ceasing round
of beginnings and endings
the countless created things.

Observant, knowing, without emotion
all good and evil, joy and sorrow
lightness and dark, now and then
contained in His circular self.

No need to choose or feel
for all possible choices
feelings, and states of being
are He, and He is them.

Worship Him
for his clear-eyed, merciless wisdom.
Pity Him
for He is not life, but only existence.

Setting Out

Spring Again

Spring arrives. With it
a seasonal disregard
for the worst-case scenario
as days unwind and my blessings
always outweigh my burdens.

Astarte's crescent arcs across
the April night
cherry trees shiver, shake themselves
petals floating past on Easter air
surviving winter pansies
glare at the world
from their altar on my terrace.

It's a new world again
right here, right now, every second
flooded with God's green beauty.
There's just no time to worry
about tomorrow.

Balch Creek Canyon

You can't step
into the same river twice
That goes for creeks in canyons, too
the water moves on and moves away.

Nor can you step
into the same canyon twice
though no Greek philosopher said so
The canyon goes on living, moves on and moves away.

All things dissolve and disappear
trees, plants and rocks departing into time
flowing like water but too slowly
for our mayfly lives to time their going.

Stripped of their green, bare-branched
the maples on the canyon bank wear moss,
Gray fur coats to warm them
till springtime comes and brings their leaves again.

Laughing liquidly, slipping over stones
the creek chatters, grumbles over
the basalt bones of the canyon
It's come this way, been here before

knows the path to the ocean
to the sky, and back again.
The canyon and its creek keep time
to many different drummers.

Things look the same each day,
But never are.

Dog Zen

Warm sun and brown dog
pull me outside
under spring skies and gray gravid clouds
not a day for indoor meditation.

Eager ferns, spring nettles
pale shoots of elderberry line the trail
gray basalt wears its rose-green lichen coat
crumbles in time with the centuries.

Snow, rain and sun fall all at once
the trail black with water, white on the verge
Cloud shavings slip from bare maples
just awakening, buds urgent.

No need for meditation if you're Sadie
brown Buddha sniffing snow and mud
Enlightenment is your nose
your tongue the universe.

It's all here;
It's all now!

Old Fish

I've lived long in these waters
grown fearsome in my solitude
feeding on what floats by
Sweet and bitter; in the end
it's all just food.

Each year more wary;
not that I haven't taken a hook before,
hidden inside the false promise
of nourishment.

But I shook it off
returned to my pool under the bridge
between the two kingdoms.

This time I may be caught
the barbéd hook sinks deep
as I pull on the patient line.

What could it be like
to leave these waters?

Wine and Bread

That first night we met,
and for some time after,
if asked to describe you
in a poetic manner
I'd have said I saw you
as a rare wine; your
deep serious self hiding
aspects that would only show
as time passes
and you open up
well structured, racy, complex
warm and full bodied on the palate
hints of lemon, strawberries, tar
asperity and fire balanced with
solid seriousness—a long finish.

If asked again, now
it's much simpler
you're my daily bread.

Angry Child

I love you
like Jesus loved Judas
not with affection
but with the deeper love we hold
for one to whom we're bound
in sacred contract.

Before I was
before any of us were
we stood before the gods
I swore with you I could live a life
in which forgiveness was stronger
than my need
for perfection in others.

So far, it's not going well
each night in the Garden I pray
for the bitter cup of my need
to be taken from me.
Each morning they bring me
my crown and cross
I am not God.
I can't forgive you
for turning your face from me.

My altar is crowded with tokens of myself.
It must be swept clean
before an offering of love
can be placed on it.

Artist's Model

She never looked beautiful
She looked like art.

Anyway
art isn't supposed to look beautiful
it's supposed to make you feel
something.

Crows

The crows of winter
sleek, sooty scavengers of the outer edges
drift rudely out of the oyster sky
and stalk the lawn
looking for food or, maybe
just the bloody amusement
of bullying a few worms
on a weekend afternoon.

It's late in the shortest month
Days are longer
the midnight blues of dawn and dusk
more widely spaced each day
His own blacks and blues
keep time with the sun as it climbs and sinks
but they have other partners
and dance with them as well.

Summer came early this year
in February, he thinks it was
And on the best of days
when he can let himself relax
into her fierce, determined love
her silver sun floats over him
and the crows, the black crows
with their blue companions
keep a wary distance.

Fire Starter

In the beginning is the word, and
in every beginning is a dangerous magic
not in the words
but in the promises
lying within them.

In a universe of words
only a few are the torch
that lights the fire.

We are children of urgent need and desire
touched by the gods our words flame forth
light the fire that consumes or heals us.

Caught between our need
and the fear of being known
we are burnt by a didactic flame
that teaches us not to learn
but to remember.

Garden of Eden

Last night, after my friends left
while I cleaned up the dishes
I put on fine young cannibals
and roland gift sang
you drive me crazy
and the years slipped away
twenty-eight of them now
and we were in your kitchen
you up on the low counter
where you kept the phone
while we fucked urgently
nothing in the world but
our breath in each other's mouths
and the whisper of Caron
at the warm base of your neck
carnations rising like steam
from a mountain hot spring
or from your hot tub
where we held each other
while the snowflakes fell
on our upturned faces
and we thought
time would stop
just for us
that we could always
be frozen in that fire
of hot water and ecstasy.

Hope, Reclaimed

When a drought first ends you discover
you've almost lost your belief
in the existence of rain
even as you stand
in its cool blessing.

Now flowers bloom
soaked and grateful.

Letting Him Go

She's rehearsed her leaving
wanted him gone
these last dead months
practiced the words and gestures
stood in front of her mirror
trying on moods
quiet sadness, anger, bleak resignation.

Imagined his stunned silence
pleas, tears, promises to change
recitals of excuses old and new
heartfelt pledge to do better.

And in the safety of her disengagement
played with alternatives
separation, reconciliation.

But she never looked beyond that
imagined moment
to the feelings that would follow the words
that would crash over
pulling her under, the sudden sick rip tide
of grief and remembrance.

Couldn't have imagined
his quick assent
and his quiet, relieved smile.

Neptune's Song

A raindrop on my window, then another
they touch and merge so easily
once-separate surfaces
now shared and singular.

You lie on me; I breathe your breath
see your sight
hearts beat together, atoms touch
but soft skin will not yield.

Leave your body. I'll leave mine
and we'll be raindrops
touch, merge, make a single ocean
evaporate by our own heat

Return to heaven
start again.

Oncidium/Dancing Lady

Brushing back her ebony hair
Miko turns, a two-step dance
kimono swirling, right hand reaching
for a branch of yellow butterflies
severs its stem
slips it in her hair
then kneels, touches my hand
laughs, and dances away again.

Post Breakup Writer's Block

No words
no combinations of words
no ideas—no thoughts at all
then and when erased
banished by the impact of now

Nothing in the tool kit
but platitudes, conclusions
time-worn adjectives—like that one—
hackneyed expressions, aphorisms
things said that, on further thought
need to be said differently
or can't, really, be said at all.

The dry dust of instant coffee
in the bottom of my cup
no scent, no aroma, no feeling, no life
no steam without the boiling water.

Repent or Perish

How, once again, was I attracted to someone
whose beauty was only surpassed
by her utter indifference
to anyone's needs
but her own.

Maybe it was a perfect match.

Sunday Morning in Goose Hollow

Leaf tinged, yellow green
Spring light peers curiously
through windows streaked with pollen
I wake up and I watch.

Watch it caress the fine blonde hairs
on her breasts and stomach
on her stomach—which rises and falls
with her steady breathing.

I watch and think about
the random sequence of events
that brought me to this late Spring morning

Caught, as always,
between gratitude for an adventure—
our two Venn diagrams overlapping
for a narrow wedge of time—
and an urgent need to be off the island
and on my way home to Ithaca.

The rhythm of her breathing shifts and shortens
she rolls towards me
eyes closed and nipples hardened and I think
one more time, mystery girl
let's love each other as much as we can.

Talking It Out

My heart is broken
I said
it could have been so much worse, she countered
I'll love you forever
I pleaded.
but how long is that, really? she asked.

If I must burn, let me burn in heaven,
I declaimed
that is not it. That is not it at all, she replied
only the dead are beautiful and free.

We are sparks in the night wind
I offered
burning the past to light our tomorrows.

We would spend a lifetime,
she concluded
arguing who was the tinder
and who the match.

Vulnerability

Relationships are like seeds
nothing grows
'til the ground is broken.

Being broken open is scary
think how the earth feels
when the farmer sets about
his springtime business.

Hood Canal September 30

A long time
since I've been on these waters

It was summer
a million stars in the black sky
an antic breeze
the lights of Belfair in the distance
the smell of just-cut hay
fireflies in the water
a freckled girl close
on the night beach.

Is that how it was? Did I say that right?
I'm not sure
the past is now another country
and I no longer speak the language

Autumn Rain

He leaves her. Leaves fall
small grief inside the great—her
tears in autumn rain.

Passion Play

Good Friday

Cherry petals drifted past unnoticed
floated silently on swirls
of warm night Easter air
stirred by passing cars and late night walkers
while we kissed; only half-aware,
and open—for a moment—
to each other.

With careful hands,
you laid your flowers down and waved goodbye
taking yourself, the moment
the soft feel of your lips on mine
all of them gone with you.

Easter Sunday

Cherry petals drifting past, unnoticed
lift silently on swirls
of late-day Easter air
stirred by passing cars and Sunday walkers
while I stand, half-aware
trying to recall—for one clear moment—
your stunned warmth.

With careful shovel
I open up the earth, for just a moment,
carefully planting your blue-eyed gift;
and some part of you is resurrected
and returns.

Along the Way

Cosmic Laughter

The most dangerous myths
 are those most comforting
"we grow," "we learn"
"it's a purpose-driven life"
I'm not so sure.

The sun returns each day
 the moon each night
 seasons come, go, and come again
 it's an eternal round
 not an ascending path to nirvana.

The truck that ran you down last time
 is here again,
 just painted a different color
 so why do we think
 we'll have better luck next time?

There may not be a next time
 just the same time, once again
 that we only recognize when
 it's in the rear view mirror and
 we've lost our chance to hit the brakes
 and make a quick right turn to another future.

It's Groundhog Day, and we have
 all eternity to figure it out
 meanwhile, there's the sound of cosmic laughter
 in a remote corner of the universe.

Father of the River

Rivers are on my mind again

The river that flows by my door
the river that flows through my mind
the river that flows through my life.

Forever arriving and departing,
they will not stay
and yet refuse to leave.

My rivers course through me
flow together, separate again
our relationship fleeting
like the half-formed intent
we bear on awakening
which subsequent seconds chase from our minds
like the coming night chases the light
from the evening sky.

I have lived on the banks of my rivers
they invite me in, but I hesitate
fear I'll lose my footing
be pulled under
yet I keep wondering what it would be like
to surrender to the flow.

He Comes, Consenting

The Greeks knew the secret
they and others who traded lives
for the favor of unyielding gods
the perfect sacrifice is one
to which the victim consents
joins willingly in the offering of themselves.

But more: the willing victim is itself
the perfect sacrifice. These others—
the priests with obsidian knives
the king seeking fair winds
to sail for battle—are accessories
to the essential act.

Led by a girl, a loose silk cord
gracing his neck, the bull
approaches the altar.

He comes willingly
knowing what others there
can only hope: That in his death
he and the god are one.

Hope Against Hope

Penelope sits before her loom
plucks the threads, unweaves her never-finished work
sets out the hand-dyed wool for morning
lapis, persimmon, the soft gray of a grieving dove
considers asphodel, but death's white flower
seems too certain—premature
he may still return.

The palace is silent
servants and children sleep
outside on black water
unseen rain and half-seen moon
a sheet of shattered light
dances on Poseidon's wine-dark surface
another evening on the boundary
between loneliness and solitude.

Twenty years weaving and unweaving
waiting to see how the story turns out
ever more certain the one who left
is not the one she waits for to return.

She reaches out her hand across the table
selects the yarn, joyful and poppy-bright
hopes it will be the color she can weave
if he returns tomorrow.

Life on the Installment Plan

I have never owned my life
—it's all on loan from the Universe anyway—
choosing instead to pay
periodically
for packages to be delivered and
opened, like Pandora's box
setting free the next mysterious chapter.

Still paying gratefully for what
I purchased in the past
still in debt to the present
the future hasn't been ordered yet
I've always been an impulse buyer.

Only in the rear-view mirror
can I see it all unfolding
with antic connectedness
and random digressions.

The old goat in me is still alive
still sniffing the electric scent
of the next best thing
in and out of love
anarchic
rebelling against boredom.

Still setting out on voyages by moonlight,
I catch my eye in the mirror
and think "not bad, you old pirate."

No Pain, No Gain

Why this perverse connection
between the blessings we're given
and the pain they bring?

Every gift from the gods
beauty, wisdom, the love of the crowd
is a loaded pistol handed to a child.

Believing our lives are bulletproof,
we see only the treacherous power
of what we've been given
after we impulsively pull the trigger
and our lives, carefully planned, well controlled
lie bleeding at our feet.

And yet:
if we don't kill that which is
how can we give birth to the terrible blessing
of what might be?

Off the Path

Never take the same path twice
life will see you coming
and trap you
in its sticky embrace.

But a morning this fine
recalls an earlier life
when dew clung to the ocotillo
and settled like diamonds
on the cactus spines.

And if I look up
I can just make out the path—
like a valley in the daybreak sky.

So I walk this valley over the city
the air is cool
looking down
I can almost remember
why I came this way again.

On Love When Freely Given

Love can be given
can be received
but cannot be bargained for
what is purchased is never truly possessed.

Love is a continuous act
a verb, active, sometimes imperative
but never a noun
never the name of something
and has no boundaries.

Loving truly, we love infinitely
not out of our own capacity
but as the essential attribute of Love itself.

At the end, everything is worn away
but love and consciousness
the act, and our knowledge of the act
and we are left, clear and sparkling
in the stream.

Paradox

These lives we inhabit—
nested parentheses
Venn diagrams
Russian dolls

Always—
sorrow inside of joy
dark swallows the light
loss is wrapped in the gift
tomorrow devours today

Grieve, joyfully, for our coming loss
for sorrow shot through with gratitude
the greatness of our grief
will be surpassed
by our joy in the beauty
of the gift
we are given.

Prayer for Compassion

Bow down before the wisdom
whose only source
is participation.

Walk with those who suffer
who have known the first words
and the endings.

Be silent. Bend your knee
before the highest wisdom
which is compassion.

And in the evening, laugh the laughter
that lingers in the half-light
of our unanswered questions.

Silence

In a place of eternal calm
I kneel before a slab of rock
at the summit of a mountain
and wait for the god of the place to speak.

The cliffs below echo with silence
peace floats up from the forest floor
mid-summer sun regards me
as just another part of the scene.

A myriad audience waits
quiet and unseen, for the message
answer me, God
but not just yet.

When I speak
when you speak through me
much is lost. Your voice is clearest
in my silence.

Song of Ourselves

We sing our songs
from light and darkness
sing and hope our voice is heard
among the calls of all the others.

But many are called
and none are chosen.

Frogs hidden in the night marsh, we
send out our voice in ragged song
call to a rumored prince unseen
who sits behind a darkened window
while we send signals through the glass.

After the hopeful music
in the indifferent silence
when the song stops
who will sing for us?

Summer Night on Wind Mountain

This night did not fall
afternoon shadows rose cautiously
crept silently up the hill
seized the day and devoured its light
what's left of the feast are the night's smells
earth, warm stone,
the crushed grasses on the summit.

Summer stars float above in
clean, infinite clarity
there's a distant hum in the heavens
it must be the background sound
of the billion suns.

Sunday Morning #2

This Sunday morning's made so fine
it makes me resent both
my mortality
and the deliberate speed of light.

Before I die, I want to see them all
the billions of created things
numberless planets and their people
I'll never see.

They're all out there, you know
waiting for our appreciation.

Let's do it now, this afternoon
we'll be back in time for a glass of wine
then some dinner and quiet conversation
about the journey.

The hard thing about living
is not that we die, but that
we die with so much of life
unlived.

The Knight Confronts the Dragon

In my stories
I'm the knight in shining armor
in truth, I'm also the dragon
victory will come
only when I slay myself.

The Midwife

Words are the enemy of feelings
deeper meanings lost
in the dictionary's shiny steel
building block certainties
write down what we feel?
try making bricks out of fog.

There's a slippery, bloody gulf between the two
feelings struggle to be born whole, expansive,
without limits
words hope to contain them
we're left with the rude newborn
twisting, squalling, raw and inarticulate.

So we swaddle them in words,
capture their bare essence, exclude
their inconvenient mystery
but meaning shifts
changes the subject like an old man
slides away, begins anew
leaves the old conversation unfinished.

In this shifting ground between the two kingdoms
I tend my brood.

The More You Pay, the More It's Worth

God, I hate this
tearing, heart-sick tension
between the soft captivity of love
and the bleak joy of being alone!

The solitary virtue of solitude:
the numb safety—
always the outsider
but never accountable
for another's needs or agenda.

I crave the warm curve
of a woman in my bed
the entertaining disorder
of her sounds and presence
in my carefully constructed life.

But every form of refuge has its price.
The cost, of either choice
cannot be calculated
and the payments never end.

This Caterpillar Life

One foot in each world?
I have them in a hundred worlds
a centipede whose feet have stepped
in all the paint pots
splashing a happy rainbow scrawl
across the graph paper of my years

Vidi Aquam

I saw water
coming forth from the canyon
coming forth from the springs
above the canyon, on the right side
coming forth from the snows
that came before.

And all for whom
the water came
drank
and their thirst was refreshed.

Give thanks for the snows
for the springs and for the water
for what was before them
for the universe
that endures forever.

Zen Christ

Feeling cosmically unloved?
Forget yourself
don't believe your unbelief.

Put on the yoke of necessity with relievéd joy
empty your pockets
give everything to the wind
then pay attention.

The love never stops coming back.

Athena

I've caught glimpses of you
so often
in that slender wedge of time
between desire and regret.

Believed, on my long journey home
you would finally show yourself
that your peace would find me.

It's been years of enchanted islands
and flawed goddesses
for each one, thinking I'd found you
I put myself on her altar
handed her my knife and a match.

And our joy was like swords
pain and delight flowing together
indistinguishable.

Is it you, this time?
shall we talk?
there is always more to ask
more to tell.

One last time, Athena;
love me as much as you can.

Dog Mountain Haiku

Here's a cosmic truth:
we are all hairs on the back
of the same black dog.

On the Nature of God's Love

Why does morning's sun strike first
the tree that's broken
by December's storm?

Crows II

Wheeling sharp-beaked shadows
an oil spill on the sunset
the raucous raven mob
mocks the quiet colors of evening
over the hills.

Their ragged calls
God's droll counterpart
to the infinite opalescence
she is busy giving birth to
in the western sky.

Nature's sense of irony
is seen best in Her contrasts
maybe the sunset wouldn't be as beautiful
without the crows.

Sometimes, I wonder
where She puts us in the picture.

Sisyphus in Hades

A sunny morning in mid-July finds me
a skeptical, resigned, unwilling captive
in Hades; disguised this time
as a conference room I would never willingly
be caught dead in; pushing uphill the rock
of my continuing education sentence
for a profession I've grown to hate.

Somewhere, unseen, but right in front of me
there's a door into summer
to the sun, the warm stones and bright sea
to a life and work blessed with light, warmth
and the certainty of significance. A life
I crave to live, but cannot find
at least it seems that way.

Seen differently, from the other side of the river,
I've found the Elysian fields
the very same life fulfilled; gifted with children, family
deep friendships, new love, my poetry, laughter
and the cool blessing of solitude
Which of these would I trade
for that which I do not have?

Or maybe that's not the right question
now how do I get out of here?

Where the Laughter Went
for Mike and Ed

It's hard to remember when it stopped
It didn't end, but sort of tapered off
like so many other things about ourselves
we seem to have mislaid over the years:

Those beer and sometimes dope-fueled evenings
of clumsy guitar music, favorite songs
and the occasional laughing jag
that left us weak and side-ached
wondering how it had all started.

Funny. We know each other now
better than we ever did
but the years of days
are stacked heavily, one on the other
the years and the days and the jobs
and the marriages and the kids
and the realization, finally
that we only had a walk-on part
and the show's almost over.

After a while, it all adds up
or it doesn't. And you're standing there
with these people you now love
more deeply than you thought possible
but the laughter, the heedless,
carefree, idiot, raucous laughter
is somehow locked away
in rooms for which
you no longer have the key.

Fear of the Dark

Good or evil?
It's a false dichotomy
no light without darkness
deny the darkness?
It will surprise and overwhelm you.

We can only guard against what we know
so we learn our shadows
not to conquer them
but to protect those we love.

Myself? I favor getting acquainted
invite them in for tea, or a stiff martini
have a conversation, spend some time
give them a name.

Naming the shadow,
we reduce it to something
that can have a name
no longer a formless malignity.

As with any new friend, ask about its fears
its feelings, hopes, and boundaries
the less strange, the less frightening
like your dimly remembered
grandfather.

Farther Along

Belated Conversation

My parents' graves
are at the top of a hill
I walk there sometimes
it's not too far
hoping for the one conversation
we were never able to have.

We're closer now than before
it isn't death, but life, that separates us
like the audience at an absurd play
we don't really understand the characters
until they've left the stage.

Their voices are faint
but clearer as the years pass
my hearing has improved
with age.

Golden Haired Lion

Another year
more companions sick or dead
as the current speeds up.

My long river of choice and chance
nears the sea
where all beginnings and ends converge
at eternity's gate
and night and day expire.

Love, once given
can be repented, can be recalled
but cannot be reclaimed
no regrets.

I am a golden-haired lion
I watch the dying sun
and remember
the furnace whispers for me
but I will not burn.

The only true sin
is forgetting.

Parapluvium

While our father was alive
we could still be children.
born after him, borne for him,
sheltered by his kindly but
sometimes distracted fatherhood
our umbrella against the rain of fate.

Now the umbrella is folded and laid away
with it, the last of our childhood
I watch the world and weather with a wary eye
all joys are infused with unspeakable knowledge
especially the joy of love for my children.

Once friendly rain clouds bear new menace,
for I am now the umbrella
—or, lightning rod, it often seems—
and know the role and destiny of such devices.

In my father's death I see the arc of my own life
coming to a close. I wonder about my ending
the good and ill that will live after me
and feel the need to sum my story up.

To seek forgiveness from those I've loved imperfectly
but with all my heart.

Straight and True

This looks like
the place I've been trying to find
all my life
feathery trees cradle greener shadows
underneath, a riot of flowers, warmth
the smell of peace.

So why stand here waiting?
the road is straight and true
the car has fuel for a long run
and I should be getting on.

But yet—
this road, this country, this time
are not made for one
they will only yield the sweetest of their secrets
to two.

And I know you're somewhere near
coming to meet me, almost here
and we'll ride side by side
for the rest of the journey.

Autumn on the River

Within each life, the little deaths
the slow tearing of ourselves
from the world in which delight lies somewhere
between boredom and confusion.

Deaths of parents, family, pets
and others loved and unloved
strength and senses dim
while habits grow fiercely stronger.

Classmates depart. The old house
is torn down for a new apartment
we struggle to keep what capacity we still hold
to love that which is other than ourselves.

Seasons hurry off the stage
stepping on each other's heels
in their unseemly haste to be on their way
to the next best thing.

Ahead, the river grumbles
falls away in soundless mist
voices from shore grow faint
those inside grow stronger.

The pace of leaving quickens
as we round the last bend
no reason to hold back.

With so much taken
there's so little left to lose.

Compulsory Zen

Memory fainter
tomorrow obscure
only this moment

Getting old. Here. Now.

Devolution

Grandmother cared for my mother
and for my mother's cousins, who were orphaned
and my mother took care of me
a nanny took care of my children
whose children now have, not children
but dogs
and doggy day care takes care of them.

Each generation has invested less
in that which follows. It makes sense
I guess.

Our attachment's usually not the same
for dogs as it is for children.
with dogs there's no hurt, no suffering
no struggle to love in spite of your brokenness
 and that of the broken thing you struggle to love.

We're not stuck for a lifetime
with that first dog; there will be others.
some more benefits—
no college tuition, no screaming matches,
no unanswered calls, no forgotten birthdays
so, why take the risk?

Wonder where this is going?
if we love our pets enough
will they eventually become the perfect children
we never, really, could have had?

Epilogue

Afterwards
I moved out and you moved on
your white orchids died in the dryness
of my failure—or was it refusal?—
to water them
like so many other things left untended
in my headlong life.

But for a heartbeat we touched
like two streams of lava
then launched our separate selves again
in our search for the land
of Happily Ever After.

Flicker Farm

Under the raw white winter sky
the delirious power of gardens dreaming
spring roses and summer honey
incubate.

We sleep in stillness
while the goddess recalls
diamond moonlight
roads in the rain
and the lazy blue days
behind the wind.

Free as a Bird

Sunset in San Miguel
a blind hummingbird vibrates urgently
against the rough plaster of my bedroom wall
the courtyard window and freedom
unseen below.

Ginny

Fifty years she's been a tailor
these days it's more about letting out waistlines
than crafting a new jacket
anyway, the clothes I have look like they'll last
as long as I do.

Stitching, cutting, sewing
deft fingers in expert motion
until last month when her hands went numb
now garments hang on the rack, untouched.

Life hasn't been kind; her husband dead
from too much retirement
and too little to do
daughter on the other side of the country
doesn't call that often.

This morning I went to see her
rhododendrons blushed by the cedar tree
a luminous blue jay pecked in the untended garden
a million tiny suns on the grass
in the mid-day rain drops.

Beauty and sorrow tangled
in all our days. How would one have meaning
without the other?

It's All Relative

The narrow moment
between knowing
and not knowing

The eternity
between not knowing
and refusing to know

Midnight in Port Alfred

In endless ranks of tired waves
the ocean probes the shore
withdraws, again defeated
sighing through the pebbles.

Wind-scattered clots of foam
skid across the midnight beach
on the south horizon
a single light rises and falls
the tide recedes, muttering to itself.

Farther south, the same night sea
breaks on frozen shores
I walk the ocean's edge
take inventory of my dwindling store of days
between now and then.

For Mike

Old Man River

Roiled swift water tumbles by
eroding clay banks overborne
Sere grasses spent,
bracken bent
stooped like old men used and torn
the residue of last week's storm.

Bare trees black with winter rain
anchor in eddies, awkward frames
once hidden by their summer leaves
a solitary sparrow grieves.

I am a river in Winter.

Rain/Dance

Easy to dance in sunlight.
bright beams slip
through massed gray clouds
strike softly
on our upturned faces.

When storms come
as they will
we still must dance. Dance while tears
mingle with the rain
tears washed away by the water,
flow out on the earth
return again to the heavens
from which we come.

Dance gratefully in the storm
dance for the seeds we are sowing
for the coming sunlight
that will nurture them.

What the waters teach—
only in the hard rain and the deep pools
do we discover our souls
pray the rain will pass
but not until its lessons
have been learned.

Route of the Cascades

Drowned green fields
bare oaks, dandelions
a green mist of new grass
implacable banks of blackberries
bare tree wearing a crown of crows
flooded land, its contours smoothed
—like the loss of memory—
the past forever detached from the present.

A gaggle of tired houseboats,
Peeling paint, moss-covered roofs—
an embarrassed, tired little sanctuary—
a solitary Holstein in a shit-filled trampled pen
watches pensively as we pass and wonders
bright promise of new turf on a country school
soccer pitch
nameless freight trains
creek banks sprinkled with garbage
like a diseased skin.

Flooded alders mirrored
rooted in the sky below them
back yards of tired towns lie in a coma
of resignation
a stream of semi-consciousness
taverns, fat-tired pickups
fishing boats on trailers in driveways
yards filled with old cars

male tokens of power
disintegrating but unabandoned.

Shotgun houses and mobile homes layered
with a thin coat of green lichen
sink slowly into the damp earth.

Still in the Orchestra

There's not much left of the song
but I tilt my head and listen
greedy for what's left
the last notes slip by like the final drops
in an upturned glass.

Poetry, always looking backward
has been my music
but emotion recalled in tranquility
is a past happiness
like a warm breeze it
leaves little trace.

There was faith,
the dull stubborn kind; mostly
a rejection of each day's truth
along the way I lost that song
but nothing has really changed
since I mislaid it.

I'm still trying to hear
the liquid lilt of the inaudible
still paging through old scores
to avoid the danger of imagining
some new arrangement.

But there's so much music waiting
and so little time.

The God and the Swan

The Ivel is a minor god
winding its narrow ancient way
across the Thames valley
choked with waving water weeds.

Under the footpath bridge
the river shrugs past me and bends round the corner
the thorny crown of its briar crusted bank
fringed with nettles.

Buckingham's birds watch motionlessly
conclude I'm not a threat
return to cropping
the river's green streamers.

The Library

Parquet floors creak with age
like an old man's knees
tattered paper bindings worn with time
stretch up from floor to ceiling.

In the center, an ancient table
and a Chinese lamp beside a high-backed chair
quiet, a scent of dust and paper;
a place to read or think, a private refuge.

This room of mismatched books contains
my life of seventy-something years
the hurts embraced and joys endured
images grim, humorous, trite and tragic.

The wins and losses, high goals and low gods
that fed and drove me down the years
all here in these books; yet, now
they seem unreal, someone else's story.

As for the details, all these books will tell
if you spend the time to take them down
and read.

But no, I've got a better thought
let's just sit here on the couch and talk.

Tucson Winter

Gray clouds piled overhead
empty stalls and trampled hay
distant thunder like horses

Mallards

Come on, Martha! This looks
pretty much like the place
we stayed last year. This curb
this grass that's just across
the street from all the houses.

No, I can't find the damned
path through the bushes to
the little pond we nested by
just keep on walking and
ignore the cars. It's here
somewhere.

And no, I won't
stop to ask directions
we didn't need directions
to fly three thousand miles
and we got here just fine.

Besides, just listen to them
we don't speak their language
and I left my phrase book
somewhere in that marsh in Mexico.

Between the Bars

He can't sign his name anymore
hands shake an up-tempo rhythm
like some damned digital drum kit
that you can't find the switch to turn it off
so Peggy does it for him.

Still, he can pick up his fiddle
squeeze the neck and draw the bow
the tremors stop
and a high thin wire of golden sound
uncoils in the room,
grateful notes spilling like drops of sunset
as they slip to freedom
between the back-beat bars
of his affliction.

Eyes closed, smiling that bad boy grin
his renegade pulse is still
and time stops
for a few short numbers.
Then he opens his eyes
hands the fiddle to Peggy
and steps off the stage.

The silent beat returns
as she closes the fiddle case.

Appointment in Samarra

I'm getting out of here
this relationship is killing me.
or maybe it's the town or this job, or the weather
or the too-familiar story
I seem to cycle through.
Whatever.

Nothing changes.
everything in the rear-view mirror
is catching up again.
past and future smeared together
a never-ending present that always brings me
circling back to where I started.

No more re-runs.
I need to switch to a new channel
need to trade in
the old familiar ending
for a new happily ever after
a new love, a new look, a new town,
a new last chance to get it right
for once and for all.

Stay or go—that's always the question—
and our answer always finds us.

Journey's End

Resurrection

Morning arrives: an insistent beggar
clutching the chilly clothes
it shuffled off in yesterday
lemon light floods under ice blue sky
we wake again, hoping salvation
arrived in the night.

We're each the center of our universe,
the world refracted through
the imperfect lens of ourselves
each night a little death
each morning we are born again.

Asleep we dream of morning
dream we'll rise, beautiful and new.

Epitaph

Past happiness leaves little trace
The ten thousand dead things
claw at our memory
old joys, old sorrows
disputes unresolved
now become unresolvable.

The dead and the living equally
unavailable to one another.

Anger, indifference and, finally, death
have placed you beyond my hope for
reconciliation.

What's left is the vengeance
of patient endurance.

The Battle of Bakhmut

Bare shattered trees, cold moonlight
The coughing of guns
Bones, barbed wire
The white faces of the dead

Cowboy Joe

I remember him first
about the time he was ten
a small cowboy
in the middle of the gang
he had on jeans, a brown plaid shirt
bare feet and a battered cowboy hat
in the wet December afternoon.

His arched eyebrow
and one-sided grin
let you know he was one of the good guys
maybe a little wild
but more Roy Rogers than Lash Larue
a musical, big-hearted cowboy
and not a gun fighter.

Like a lot of cowboys
he had a difficult relationship
with his horse
it got him there and got him home
but it was an uncontrollable, mean son of a bitch
and bucked and bit him all too often.

As they both grew older
it got harder to handle,
even as he needed it more
But he kept on riding it, he said
because it always took him home
when he was lost.

He's gone now
but you can still hear the music he made
if you're quiet and listen.
And you can still feel his grin
in the love of those he left behind.

Darkness Falls

Razor wire
troops in DC
children in cages.

Who wins?

Death Haiku

Death is an illusion
an actor leaving the stage
for a costume change

Free Advice

Out of the wrinkled grey afternoon
into the desperate chatter of the wake
for a last look where he lay
in his coffin.

I heard him say:
"It's the bleak virtues that are the measure—
loyalty, persistence, joy in the small things
most of all, that you keep on smiling
when all the idiot romance is burned away
by endless days of just getting by

And you finally own the despair you saw
around the edges of your parents' eyes,
when you could bring yourself to look."

For Lucretius

The gods are finally dead
departed under an empty sky darker than evening
nothing of the sun remains
but bruised clouds
and bitter cobalt rain

All things go to the grave
and so with each of us
worn out by the long years
borne by the weeping
that walks only with death

But life persists
morning arrives with its bright lances
pours out the new day
from Apollo's bowl
and the funeral chant is mingled
with the cries of newborns
coming to this world of light.

Jim

He was loved
by his family—by his wife, children, grandchildren
and by a wider circle
a circle whose blurred boundaries never quite
excluded anyone who met him.

In these last ten years he had
all the virtues he needed:
first, kind good humor about himself.
for the rest of it, patient acceptance,
submission, resignation
and, without fail, joyful courage.

Like a familiar jacket, and always with good humor
he put on each one as needed for the day's weather
and held up a hopeful light
for a journey begun far too soon.

Last Train Home

The empty station sighs
with the soft swish of the janitor's broom
and echoes with the absence
of old companions gone ahead.

The solitary traveler finds
a late-day journey has its solace
a book and gently waning sunlight
are the kindest of companions
along the way towards evening darkness.

In time I hear the boarding call
step out to the platform
surprised to find another traveler
this late in my now shared evening
and walk towards the empty car.

Shall we sit together
for the rest of the journey?

The Harvest

Over a few seasons
we planted the two of you
on a hill with others
whose fruitful days had passed.

There's no escape from necessity:
each generation is spent
in the care and feeding of its crop
while the next, unripe, plants its own seeds.

You never knew, really,
what you engendered;
and we're still living the answers
but I think you knew enough to be satisfied
ready to be ploughed under
when it was time.

Did you notice the irony?
God loves her cosmic jokes
even the solace of physical love
was a trick, resulting in more
of what some said
you already had too many of.

But I think you got it right
eight seeds sprouted before your work was done
one cut down early; the others rangy
idiosyncratic, bearing their own unique fruit

exotic variations in the field you fertilized.
who would have thought
what was in your seed, in your egg?

Until you brought us forth
and now it's our turn.

Better Luck Next Time

Death calls. Just then
that trickster Enlightenment appears
smiles his best Mona Lisa.

Epilogue

Well, there you have it. Those are the feelings, expressed in words and images that offered themselves this time around, and I offer them to you. But no answers are given. Like the Greeks at Troy, I've moved my troops up to the walls of the city, hoping to take it by force. The gates, however, remain stubbornly closed.

Colophon

The text of this book is set in Adobe Jenson Pro. Titles are set in Myriad Standard.

Adobe Jenson Pro is based on a design created by Nicolas Jenson. It is an old-style serif typeface drawn for Adobe Systems by Robert Slimbach, Adobe's chief type designer. Nicolas Jenson, who was born about 1420 in Sommevoire, Champagne, and died in Rome in 1480, was a printer and publisher who developed the roman-style typeface. He studied printing under Johannes Gutenberg in Mainz before opening a printing shop in Venice.

Myriad Standard is a humanistic type in the Adobe Originals series. It was designed by Robert Slimbach and Carol Twombly with Fred Brady and Christopher Slye and was first released in 1992. It is used for both display and text.